Be a Critical Thinker

Hone Your Mind to Think Critically

Revised Edition

Donald L. Karshner

Copyright © 2014 by Donald L. Karshner
Revised Edition

All Rights Reserved

Published by Bullen Publishing Services

Publisher's Cataloging-in-Publication data

Karshner, Donald L.
Be a Critical Thinker : Hone Your Mind to Think Critically / Donald L. Karshner
p. cm.
ISBN 978-0-615-78374-1
1. Critical Thinking — Handbooks, manuals, etc. 2. Thought and Thinking — Study and Teaching. 3. Problem Solving. I. Karshner, Donald L. II. Title.
B441.K37 2013
153.4'2--dc23

ISBN 978-0-615-78374-1

Library of Congress Control No: 2013936195

For more information, please visit
http://bullenpublishingservices.com.

Editor: Martha M. Bullen, Bullen Publishing Services
Cover and interior designer: Deana Riddle, BookStarter

Book cover art: Photograph of Auguste Rodin's sculpture, The Thinker

Printed in the United States of America

Dedicated to my children,

W. Christen and Donald L, Jr.

My granddaughters, Alexandra and Carolyn

and my great-grandchildren, Tyler, Trevor,
Kendal and Trey

PREFACE

I have surprised myself in writing this book. I hope you – the Reader-Thinker – will discover your own surprises as well.

How did this book come about? I remember teachers in high school, college, and graduate school who encouraged their students to be critical thinkers. Vividly, I remember some of my teachers presented provocative ideas that could be applied in order to become such a thinker. I have incorporated many of the ideas that I have remembered in this book. However, in reflecting on my education, I have concluded that it's easier to exhort students to become critical thinkers than to present helpful ways to accomplish this goal.

During the early years of my chosen profession, it did not take me long to realize that I needed to hone my thinking process to become a more honest and truthful thinker. Through the years I would jot down ideas heard on the radio or television, and would clip out quotations or articles found in newspapers and magazines that I thought might help me to become a more astute thinker. I would place these items in an envelope and reviewed them upon occasion.

I recommend that you purchase a manila envelope and begin collecting materials that could help you become a more proficient thinker. Place in the envelope anything from various sources that may help you to be a critical thinker. Examples include book reviews, articles, quotations, comments, cartoons, jokes, newspaper clippings, magazines, etc.

When my older granddaughter enrolled in college, I casually asked her if she might find it helpful if I were to write down some ideas which she could use in writing reports, essays, or book reviews. She agreed to my suggestion. Later, she told me that not only had she found them helpful, she had reviewed them several times. What more encouragement could a grandfather receive than that? I reasoned if she found my suggestions helpful, perhaps others might find them beneficial as well. This book evolved from the few pages I presented to my granddaughter.

I want to thank my family, friends, and teachers whose lives have been open books of intelligence and reason. They have helped me beyond measure to be honest and questing, respecting both questions and differences of opinion.

Also, I wish to express my gratitude to scores and scores of people whom I have heard over the airways or who have been authors of articles or books for inspiring me to become a more honest thinker. I regret to say that most are now nameless to me, but they have not been forgotten. To all I say, thank you!

The original manuscript for *Be A Critical Thinker* was handwritten. The first two friends who tried to read my writing were C. Scott Trull and Sheldon Strober. They found my penmanship challenging. After reading the original copy, they encouraged me to continue. Their encouragement motivated me to finish my project.

The next task was to try to translate my writing to typed pages. Douglas Rorapaugh accomplished the almost impossible, while making many helpful suggestions and comments.

Robert Casey answered the call to read it critically. His legal mind did a masterful job in helping me to rethink several issues. His comments helped to make the book more accurate and purposeful.

Maureen Piston took on the yeoman's job of typing and preparing the book for publication. There was a first edition and a major reorganization and rewrite for a second edition. With degrees in journalism and library science, she was a perfect match for the task. She chased down quotations. Her patience was a marvel in making changes and more changes in the manuscript. Her comments were to the point. Everything she did was accomplished with excellence. I will always be indebted to her.

Proofreading involves a special talent. Scott Trull's keen mind and quick eye caught overlooked discrepancies not found by other eyes, while also making helpful suggestions.

I would also like to thank librarian Patricia L Palmer, who provided Cataloging-in-Publication data for the copyright page. I appreciate her taking the time to research and compile this helpful information for librarians.

The cover and interior design of *Be a Critical Thinker:* I visualized the cover being a vibrant green to symbolize growth and the ability to think critically. Also, I visualized an image on the cover of Rodin's sculpture The Thinker to inspire, improve and sharpen the thinking process. Along with an attractive, readable interior design, Deana Riddle has graphically and beautifully achieved these goals.

My editor and publishing consultant, Martha M. Bullen, is doing what she was meant to be and to do. She loves what she does. I found her enthusiasm contagious and inspirational. She is superbly knowledgeable and has an amazing grasp of the details of publishing. Always professional, with a keen sense of propriety, she has brought my eight-year project – the publishing of *Be a Critical Thinker* – to completion. I am profoundly grateful and deeply appreciative to you, Martha Bullen. I salute you for a job well done.

Friendship is a gift. To my friends who helped in so many ways to write this book, you are a gifted team. Thank you. I am deeply grateful to each one of you.

Philadelphia
September 2014

PART ONE

A Process for Critical Thinking

PART TWO

Supplements to a Process for Critical Thinking

PART ONE

A Process for Critical Thinking

Thoughts to Ponder to Prepare for
Reading *Be a Critical Thinker*

The Purpose of Critical Thinking

Preparation for Critical Thinking

A Process for Critical Thinking

Conclusion

The Parable of the Three Toads

Thoughts to Ponder to Prepare for Reading
Be a Critical Thinker

- "(He) has nothing to say and says it." (Attributed to Ambrose Bierce)

- "(He is) always certain, often wrong." (Adapted Latin expression)

- "I'm often wrong, but never in doubt." (Ivy Baker Priest)

- "If you can't dazzle them with your brilliance, then baffle them with your blarney." (Irish proverb)

- "Today a peacock, tomorrow a feather duster." (An adage)

- "I cannot hear what you say for listening to what you are." (Attributed to Robert Louis Stevenson)

- "The lady doth protest too much, methinks." (Shakespeare, *Hamlet*, Act III, Scene II)

- "Thou shalt not bear false witness against thy neighbor." (traditional version)

  "You shall not be a false witness." (contemporary version) (The Ninth of the Ten Commandments)

- "How a man wins tells something of his character. How he loses tells all of it." (George Strode)

- "A giraffe is an animal that looks like it had been put together by a committee." (An adage)

- "Painting stripes on a horse does not make it a zebra." (An adage)

- "Until the lions have their own historians, the history of the hunt will always glorify the hunter." (Chinua Achebe)

- "Power tends to corrupt, and absolute power corrupts absolutely." (Lord Acton)

- "To update Pascal by way of Thomas Nagel, 'If nothing matters, then it doesn't matter that nothing matters.' But if something *does* matter, we had better find out what it is. And if we don't know whether we can figure that out, we are better off betting that we can and go on looking, because if we win that bet, it could be really important, and if we lose it, it doesn't matter anyway." (W. Russ Payne)

Reader-Thinker: What matters to you?

The Purpose of Critical Thinking

The purpose of critical thinking is to scrutinize ideas and facts, even when they are inconsistent or contradictory, and to analyze interpretations that differ from other interpretations.

By applying the skills of critical thinking, you will be better equipped to clarify your thinking process, to intelligently critique what you read and hear, to correct errors, to dispel misunderstandings and ignorance, and to make a positive contribution to a discussion or debate.

NOTE: Critical thinking may be called analytical thinking. Also, critical thinking may involve creative thinking; conversely, creative thinking may involve critical thinking.

Preparation for Critical Thinking

How can you prepare to apply critical thinking to an assignment, project, or task? Begin by giving yourself the freedom and permission to be a critical thinker. Approach the process with a positive and open, inquiring mind. Vow to be creative by being innovative. Ask yourself, "In what ways can I be creative with new ideas and plans?" The fountain of creativity never runs dry.

Keep in mind that excellent research is a form of truth telling. Vow to know your subject.

Realize that just because something is said or written, it does not necessarily follow that it is valid and accurate, misleading or false. To determine these qualities is the task of critical thinking. There is no substitute for knowledge, honesty, and truthfulness.

Respect words. Be able to define, understand, clarify, and interpret words and terms. Know what they symbolize and point toward. Understand what emotions they may evoke. Appreciate the nuances that surround them. Aim for verbal accuracy.

The critical thinking process described in this book is *a* process, not *the* process. It is an avenue to test the authenticity and applicability of whatever is being considered. It can be adapted for a particular interest or assignment. It can be used in conjunction with another critical process, decision making process or planning process. What is essential is this: whatever the process, it must be honest and thorough, demanding vigorous thinking.

This critical process has been designed to be used by an individual for his or her own purposes. In addition, it may be used by groups, teams, or committees as a joint approach to dealing with problems and issues.

Reader-Thinker: Are you ready to begin? Do you have some feelings of excitement in trying to make sense of the barrage of information confronting you? By using this critical process, step by step, point by point, you may be able to understand, clarify and analyze data, facts, opinions, interpretations, beliefs, etc.

Most importantly – always
DARE TO THINK!

A Process for Critical Thinking

The Assignment, Project, Problem, Task, etc.

Make a commitment to the assignment, project, problem, issue or task. Be able to define, understand, clarify, and explain it in detail.

The Art of Asking Questions

The technique of asking questions is simple and direct. It is an art – a learned art. Underlying every assignment, project, or task are a thousand and one questions waiting to be asked. Every section or component of an assignment needs to be bombarded with questions. In fact, questions need to be pounded with other questions. Use questions to:

> understand
>
> clarify
>
> examine
>
> explore
>
> probe
>
> challenge
>
> find answers and solutions
>
> etc.

3

By asking questions, issues may be opened and concerns expressed. Intense questioning can be used to refine an assignment. It may be that a critical process may need to be used to determine whether or not some questions and responses are appropriate, relevant or applicable. Some of the questions and responses may need to be recorded and organized in order to become an integral part of the process. Later, they may be integrated into the conclusion, summary or report.

During the process for critical thinking, you may continue to ask questions by using the questions found in the Second Supplement.

Collect Data and Information

Set out to illuminate the assignment. This may be as simple as looking up a definition of a word, or it may be extensive and involved, requiring that you consult various sources for all the information needed. From this research, expect to be able to frame the issues and outline the debate.

Evaluate the Data and Sources

Recognize the necessity of continuously evaluating the data and sources. The authenticity of your assignment will rest upon the trustworthiness of the data. You may have to subject some of the data (perhaps all of it) to a critical process before they can be accepted for the assignment. Remember: critical thinking is a demanding exercise.

Criteria

Select and enumerate the criteria, standards, or qualifications for evaluating the issue, project or assignment. This procedure should be continuous–adding some criteria, subtracting others, and modifying still others. Some criteria may have to undergo a critical process before they can be fully accepted for the assignment. A variety of sources may need to be consulted in arriving at the criteria, standards or qualifications. Reminder: an evaluation of the sources of the criteria may be as important as the criteria themselves.

Priorities

Select and arrange the various components or elements of the assignment in order of priority. This simple procedure can help to give direction and purpose to the project.

What are the Assumptions?

Proceed with your assignment by listing all of the assumptions being made. In fact, it is important to realize that every component of the project or task is rooted in assumptions. Ask yourself, "What are the assumptions?" "What am I assuming?" "What are others assuming?"

What are the Implications?

Move on in the process by understanding what is being implied. Look for direct as well as indirect implications, suggestions and hints. These need to be enumerated in order to illuminate the assignment.

What are the Ramifications?

Advance in the process for your assignment by dealing with the ramifications. Ask yourself, "Where is it leading?" "Where are the branches branching out?" "Where are the tributaries flowing?" Follow the outstretching of the branches; follow the flow of the tributaries. These need to be followed, explored and evaluated. List and understand the ramifications in order to have a thorough grasp of the assignment or project.

What are the Consequences?

The next step is to list all of the consequences, possible effects, and results as they pertain to your assignment. Be specific. Some of the consequences may need to be clarified by using the critical process. You may start by asking:

What are the positive consequences, effects, results or impact?

What are the negative consequences?

What are the expected consequences?

What are the unexpected consequences?

What are the intended consequences?

What are the unintended consequences?

What are the desired consequences?

What are the undesired consequences?

What are the appropriate consequences?

What are the inappropriate consequences?

What are the realistic consequences?

What are the unrealistic consequences?

What are proper consequences?

What are improper consequences?

What are the ethical consequences?

What are the unethical consequences?

What are the legal consequences?

What are the illegal consequences?

Etc.

What are the Exceptions?

List, explore and analyze the exceptions or possible exceptions for your ideas or assignment. There may be some ideas, perceptions, purposes and plans that are irregular, distorted, or simply do not fit. All of these need to be accounted for before the task is finished.

What are the Limitations?

List the limitations, boundaries, parameters, or restraints as they emerge while using the critical process. These need to be understood before the assignment is concluded.

Safeguards

Sometimes "fences" need to be built and "guardrails" constructed. At times safety measures need to be taken because of the nature of the assignment. They may be material, physical, financial, economic, political, legal, psychological, medical, etc. The purpose and nature of safeguards need to be understood and evaluated.

Conclusion

The assignment, task, or project is finished. What difference will it make? What do you or your committee intend to do with it? How do you plan to share the information that has been assembled? What kind of response are you planning to make?

The response may be as simple as making a telephone call or sending an email. A single page may be sufficient for a particular summary, conclusion, explanation or interpretation. On the other hand, a report may require a volume containing many pages. The report may contain recommendations, policies, methods to be followed, plans for implementation, plans for action, target dates, legal opinions, statistical charts, plans for review, evaluations, etc.

The summary, conclusion, explanation, interpretation, or report should reflect the entire critical process. It will have passed through the fires of critical thinking and should reflect the light of those fires. The immediate task is to calibrate and integrate the results of the critical process. The summary, conclusion, explanation, interpretation or report should be clear, concise, understandable, thorough and exact.

The Parable of the Three Toads

During the process for critical thinking...

If you have to swallow three toads,

SWALLOW THE

BIGGEST ONE

FIRST!

Reader-Thinker: Step by step, point by point, you have applied the critical process to your ideas, assignments, projects, etc. Along the way, how many big "toads" have you had to swallow? How many little "toads?"

PART TWO

Supplements to
A Process for Critical
Thinking

1. Applying Critical Thinking to Words, Terms, Phrases, Expressions, etc.

2. More about Using Questions for Critical Thinking and a Critical Process

3. The Riddle of the Venus Flytrap

4. Applying Critical Thinking and a Critical Process to Data, Information and Evidence

5. Applying Critical Thinking and a Critical Process to Your Own Thinking and Attitudes, or to the Thinking and Attitudes of a Committee, Group or Team

6. An Evaluation of the Critical Process for an Assignment, Project or Task

7. Reflections and Suggestions for Applying Critical Thinking and a Critical Process

8. Thoughts and a Challenge

Applying Critical Thinking to Words, Terms, Phrases, Expressions, etc.

The following list provides many examples and a variety of expressions that can be submitted to a critical or analytical process. Behind each word or underlying each expression there are issues waiting to be discovered, spelled out, or translated into some form in order to be critically examined.

An absolute

An abusive statement

An accusation

An action

An addiction

An address

An advertisement, commercial or political

Advice, personal or legal

An affirmation

An agreement

An amendment

An American dream

An analysis

An angry statement

An answer

Anti-democratic beliefs, patterns and practices

Apocalyptic, catastrophic, cataclysmic thinking

An apology

An argument

An assertion

An assumption

An attitude

A bias

A biography

A bizarre statement

A blog

A blurb

A book

A budget, total or a part thereof; an increase or decrease

A buzzword

A by-law

A caricature

A cartoon

A case study

A catch phrase

A change

A chapter of a book

A character

Civil disobedience, an act of

A clash, such as a personality clash

A cliché

A closure

A command

A complaint

A compulsion

A concern

A conclusion

A conscience statement

A consequence

A conservative statement or argument

A conspiracy

A conspiracy theory

A constitution, or parts thereof

A construction project

A contract

A correspondence

A court decision

A covenant

A creed

A criterion or criteria

A criticism

A critique

A critique of a critique

A culture

Datum/Data

A debate

A decision

A defaming statement (defamation)

A defense's case

A demagogic statement

Democracy

Democratic process, The

A demonizing statement

A derogatory statement

Determinism, any type or form

A diagnosis

A diatribe

A dictum

A disagreement

A discipline

A dispute or disputation

A dissertation

A doctrine or dogma: economic, political or religious

A document

A dogmatic statement or argument

Economic mythologies

An economic theory or issue

An editorial

An episode

An ethical/moral statement

An example

An excuse

An executive order or policy

An expectation

An explanation

An explanation of an explanation

An experiment

An exposé

An extreme statement

A fable

A fact

Fanaticism, any form or type

A fictitious statement

A fight

A fixation

A forecast

A framework

A generalization

A glib statement

A goal

Gossip

A government, any form or type

A grievance

Half-truths

A harangue

A historical event, past or present

A historical issue or concern

A hymn

A hypocritical statement

A hypothesis

An idea

An ideology

An implication

An incantation, economic, political, or religious

An inquisition

An intention

An interest, as in a concern

The Internet

An interpretation of anything or an event

An interpretation of an interpretation

An intolerant statement

An issue

Jargon

A jeering statement

Jingoism or a jingoistic remark or statement

A joke

A judge's decision

A judgment

A jury's decision

A label for a person

A law

A lecture

A legend

A letter

A letter to the editor

A liberal statement or argument

A libretto

A lie

A lobbyist's purpose and plan

A magazine article

Majority rule: purpose and benefits

Majority rule: limitations and restrictions

Majority rule: rights and responsibilities, etc.

A manifesto

A memoir

A message

A method

A minority: rights and responsibilities, etc.

A minority opinion

A mission statement

A misunderstanding

A moral position

A motto

A movie

Name-calling

A negotiation

A newspaper article

A novel

An objection

An obnoxious statement

An opera

An opinion

23

An ordinance

An organization

An outlandish statement

An outrageous statement

A paradox

A paragraph

A pardon

A parody

A penalty

A phobia

A pigeonhole for a person

A plan, any type

A play

A poem

A policy

A political dirty trick

Political mythologies

A political platform, or a plank of a political platform

A political theory or issue

24

A position or stance

A position paper

A prayer

A prediction

A prejudiced statement

A premise

A principle

A problem

A procedure

A progressive statement or argument

Propaganda

A proposition

A prosecution's case

A protest

A proverb

A provocative statement

A purpose

A question

A questionnaire

A radical statement or argument

A ramification

A rant

A reaction

A rebuttal

A regulation

A reinterpretation

A rejection

A religion

A remark

A remedy

A renunciation

A report

A research project

A response

A result

A retaliation

A review of art, music, a play, movie, book, etc.

A ridiculous statement

A rule

A rumor

A scenario

A scene

A sentence (of words)

A sentence, as in a judicial sentence

A sermon

A slogan

A smear or a smear campaign

A social issue

A social service program

A solution, especially economic or political

A song

A sound bite

A statement and counterstatement

A statute

A story

A strike

A summary

A survey of questions and responses

A system

A tax plan

A term paper

A test

A test case

A theory

A thesis

A threat

A tirade

A topic

Trash talk

A treaty

A trend

A trial

A truth

An ultimatum

A vague statement

A verdict

Verses, narratives, and stories of sacred texts

A vindictive statement

Whistle blower, an act by a

A witch hunt

Reader-Thinker: It is my hope that you have been tantalized by this varied list of suggestions that can be analyzed using a critical process. Now you are invited to make a list of projects, ideas, plans, etc., that you wish to submit to the critical process.

More about Using Questions for Critical Thinking and a Critical Process

Not all questions will apply to a specific assignment. At first, lean toward the side of asking questions that you may not find applicable. You may be surprised by your ability to discover new insights when you ask this type of question.

Are you using original or secondary sources? Are original sources (also called primary sources) available? Note and record whether or not a source is primary or secondary. Accurate and trustworthy research requires this.

Are you able to trace the...

original source?

original interpretation or conclusion?

logical sequence?

chronological sequence?

historical sequence of events?

Is the sequence correct?

Are you able to draw a timeline?

Are you able to match a person to his or her times, beliefs, ideas, purposes, plans and actions of a particular period of history?

Are you using an interpretation of an interpretation? A distinction needs to be made between an original interpretation and an interpretation of another interpretation.

Ask questions to raise questions:

Did he actually say that?

Did she mean that?

Are you sure of the facts?

Is that an exact quotation?

Always be ready to ask for a definition or clarification of words and terms:

What is being defined?

What is being redefined?

What is being interpreted?

What is being reinterpreted?

Who is the who?

What is the what?

When is the when?

Where is the where?

Why is the why?

How is the how?

What did he or she know?

When did he or she know it?

How did he or she know?

Why did he or she know?

What did he or she do?

What did he or she not do?

What did he or she say or not say?

Who said what?

Who said what about whom?
What happened?
What did not happen?

What can be ruled in?

What can be ruled out?

What cannot be ruled out?

What is the premise?

What is the inference?

What is the hypothesis?

What is the thesis?

What is the antithesis?

What is the synthesis?

What is the authority for it?

Are you using deductive reasoning or inductive reasoning?

What is your...

vision?

orientation?

prerequisite?

perception?

perspective?

preconception?

conception?

What are you...

presuming?

assuming?

presupposing?

precluding?

prejudging?

What is...

explicit?

implicit?

What is the...

focus?

point?

objective?

goal?

What is the...

foundation or basis?

context?

circumstance?

Is something being placed in its proper historical, situational or circumstantial context?

What is the cause?

What is the root cause?

What are the symptoms?

What is the difference between cause and symptom?

What is the common ground?

What is the middle ground?

Where is the center?

Where is the mid-point?

Where are the extreme ends?

What is the alternative?

What are the...

    options?

    choices?

    possibilities?

What are the...

    ambiguities?

    confusions?

    inconsistencies?

    contradictions?

    paradoxes?

Is there a gap between perception and reality?

Is there a gap between expectations and reality?

Is there a difference between myth and reality?

What is being changed?

What is being transformed?

What is remaining the same?

Can it be...

    correlated?

    calibrated?

    corroborated?

    integrated?

    synchronized?

Are there parallels?

Are there patterns?

Is it balanced?

Where is the tipping point causing something to fall off balance?

Is it proportional?

Is it disproportional?

Are you making a false dichotomy between A and B?

Does something need to be standardized?

Does something need to be replaced with something else?

Is something being...

    preempted?

annulled?

subverted?

subsumed?

imposed or superimposed?

coerced?

usurped?

Is something...

overvalued?

undervalued?

an overstatement?

an understatement?

being assigned too much importance?

being assigned too little importance?

being assigned too much weight or significance?

being assigned too little weight or significance?

Is it...

an oversimplification?

an oversimplified cause and effect?

a baseless generalization?

an unsubstantiated generalization?

an exception to a generalization?

Is it...

supplementary?

complementary?

Is there a...

conflict?

potential conflict?

imagined conflict?

real conflict?

Is the conflict constructive or destructive?

Can a destructive conflict be turned into a constructive or productive conflict? How? Be specific.

Is there an unusual juxtaposition of ideas, facts or events?

Is it...

  a platitude?

  the status quo?

  a catch-22?

Does it have...

  a placebo effect?

  a bromide effect?

Is it a band-aid?

Are you universalizing something that should be localized?

Is something being localized that should be universalized?

Are you making a universal generalization without qualification, reservation, or exception? What might be a qualification, generalization, or exception?

When should a generalization become a particularity?

When should a particularity become a generalization?

When should a particularity remain a particularity?

Are you using a *both/and* when you should be using an *either/or*?

Are you using an *either/or* when you should be using a *both/and*?

Is it unique? In what ways?

What is being affirmed? Confirmed?

What is being negated or depreciated?

What is the best-case scenario?

What is the worst-case scenario?

What are the cultural influences?

What are the countercultural influences?

Do you need to have a closure about something related to your assignment, project or task?

Some Concluding Questions

Is the solution big enough for the problem? Explain.

What might be a larger problem or issue not being considered?

Are you able to match virtue to necessity or need?

Does the need surpass the supply?

If appropriate, how do you plan to deal with a disparity between need and supply?

Does the solution worsen or escalate the problem?

Is the solution based on tight or loose reasoning?

What unanswered questions might there be?

What possible complications might there be?

What positive and constructive responses might there be?

What antagonistic, negative, destructive or misleading responses might there be?

What might be remaining issues and problems?

What repercussions might there be? What type? From whom? For whom? For what purpose?

Are you able to measure the results? What

methods do you plan to use?

How do you plan to evaluate the results? Explain the methods.

How do you plan to get from here and now to then and there? Explain.

Reader-Thinker: Are there additional questions that you wish to include or ask?

The Riddle of
the Venus Flytrap

Have you ever watched

a Venus Flytrap

snare

a fly

And slowly consume it?

And then asked,

Why?

Why?

Reader-Thinker: Have you learned to ask why? Are you learning to ask why of the why?

Applying Critical Thinking and a Critical Process to Data, Information and Evidence

As you begin to deal with data, information or evidence pertaining to your assignment or task, be ready to ask yourself:

What constitutes adequate and credible data, information or evidence in order to make a trustworthy generalization, explanation, interpretation, summary, conclusion, or evaluation?

How do you determine the sufficiency of and the quality of the data, information or evidence that is necessary to make a trustworthy generalization, explanation, interpretation, conclusion, or evaluation?

What criteria are you planning to use for evaluating the adequacy and credibility of the information or evaluation?

Move ahead by studying the data, information or evidence. Listen to it. Let it speak to you. Let the generalizations, explanations and interpretations rise from the data, information or evidence. Do not impose prejudiced, preconceived ideas or a hidden agenda on the information.

Look for structures rising from the data, information or evidence. Are the structures being built on a firm foundation? Or are they being built on a limited, weak or inadequate foundation?

Are there mixed messages rising from the data, information or evidence? How can you clarify these mixed messages?

Are you looking in the wrong places for information or evidence?

Are you exaggerating or using superlatives in describing some information? Do you need to give an injection of reality to your descriptions?

Are you interpreting data, information or evidence negatively when it should be interpreted positively? Are you interpreting it positively when it should be interpreted according to its weakness or inadequacy?

Have you placed valued data, information or evidence in an incorrect context?

Do you need to consider other variables or factors?

Does something need to be added, subtracted or revised?

Have you in any way compromised some of the data, information or evidence?

How do you plan to explain or interpret the absence of, the silence of, or a gap of data, information or evidence?

It is essential to evaluate the source or sources of the criteria being used in explaining or interpreting the absence, the silence, or gap of data, information or evidence.

It is important to identify the criteria that are being assumed or are being used to explain or interpret the absence, silence or the gap of data, information or evidence.

It may be necessary to submit (a) the sources of the criteria, (b) the criteria, and (c) the explanation and interpretation of the absence, silence or gap to a critical analysis and process for clarification.

The burden of proof rests with those persons who explain and interpret the absence, silence or gap of data, information or evidence.

How do you plan to deal with data, information or evidence that leads to conclusions that you did not anticipate or expect, or that continue to elude you?

How do you plan to deal with unresolved issues revolving around the data, information or evidence?

How do you plan to deal with complications or contradictions that have arisen?

Is your conclusion rising from and emerging from the data, information or evidence?

Are you satisfied with the explanation, conclusion, etc? If yes, why? If not, what do you plan to do about it?

Reader-Thinker: What additional issues or concerns regarding data, information or evidence do you think need to be considered pertaining to your assignment or task?

Applying Critical Thinking and a Critical Process to Your Own Thinking and Attitudes, or to the Thinking and Attitudes of a Committee, Group or Team

Reader-Thinker: The following questions and comments are directed to you, and when appropriate, to members of a committee managing an assignment, project or task.

What boundaries are you willing to set for yourself in order to remain true to your values and integrity? Write them down.

It is important to understand your authority (and the authority of others) related to your assignment. Be certain to understand your specific authority: the source, its nature, purpose, expectations, responsibilities, accountability and the procedures for review and evaluation. Also, it is essential to understand the limits of your authority as well as that for others.

Is your thinking part of the problem or the solution?

Is your thinking an obstacle to the solution?

Do you acknowledge the problem but reject the solution?

Is your thinking perpetuating the problem?

Is your solution in search of a problem?

What are some of the attitudes and abilities necessary in order to be a problem-solver and a solution-maker? Write them down.

Do you have the ability to think big and to entertain large, expansive concepts? Grade yourself. If needed, what can you do to improve these skills?

"The devil is in the details." Are you able to handle details without being a micromanager, nitpicker or control freak? Grade yourself. If needed, what can you do to improve your ability to manage details?

There are occasions when it is necessary to think inside a box. There are times when the box needs to be kicked over. After you have overturned the box, what are your plans? Test them by using a critical process.

There are situations when it is essential to think institutionally or bureaucratically. But there are times when you have to step outside and gasp for fresh air. After you have filled your lungs with fresh air, what do you plan to "breathe out" on the situation? Test your plans.

Are you a bull in a china shop? Are you a full-time bull? Or a part-time bull? Pause and drink a cup of tea from a china cup at the china shop. Pause again and think. Then think some more. What are you thinking about? Test it.

Have you painted yourself into a corner? Are you planning to stay there until the paint dries? How can you exit without getting "paint" all over yourself? Test your plans.

Have you fallen into a ditch of "what if, what if" or "if only, if only?" Climb out of the ditch. Accept the challenge. Find a solution and solve the problem. Test your ideas.

Are you dazzled by the beauty of the icing on the cake? The real issue is: What are the ingredients of the cake? What is the content underlying the beautiful icing?

Do you have a tendency to see issues and problems through:

rose-tinted spectacles

grey-tinted glasses

red-colored lenses

green-colored lenses?

You may be able to see through clear lenses if you use a critical process for understanding and clarifying ideas, issues and problems.

Are you trying to transform a potato into a peach?

Reader-Thinker: You may apply this bit of agricultural wisdom as you wish. If it makes you smile, keep smiling.

Are you part of an establishment? Is it a stumbling block, or can it be of assistance? How do you plan to explain your role as a member of an establishment to others working on the assignment? How can you make your membership in an establishment become productive for the assignment?

Do the means justify the end?

Does the end justify the means?

How are you able to justify whatever you are trying to justify? What criteria can you use to make a justification?

Are you attempting to justify the unjustifiable?

Are you able to defend your assignment, project or task? How do you plan to do this? Or is it indefensible?

Are you making a claim that you cannot authenticate?

Are you making short-term decisions that may jeopardize long-term goals?

Are you stretching the truth or are you attempting to "improve" the facts?

Do you claim more for the truth or facts than they reveal or are observed?

Are you trying to make one size fit all? Are you attempting to find a single answer that will fit all situations?

Are you looking for one piece of information when you need to be looking for several pieces that should be considered?

Are you staying on the subject or are you veering off on a tangent? When can tangential thinking be an obstacle? When can it be creative and productive?

Is your thinking compartmentalized? Are you able to introduce two or three new ideas to the compartment?

How do you think you could pursue and achieve excellence with less? Less means less of anything pertaining to your assignment, project or task. Make a response.

Are you interested only in your own self-interest and in grinding your own axe?

Are you championing issues that are not relevant to your assignment?

Are you playing out a subterfuge to escape real issues?

Are you obscuring real issues instead of facing them?

Are you skirting around difficult issues or problems?

Are you secretive or hypocritical about something related to the assignment?

Are you deceiving yourself about something related to the assignment?

Is your response a resistance response?

Are you causing a paralysis of analysis? What do you need to do to break through to a conclusion or solution?

Are you able to identify a disconnect? Be specific about your responses.

Are you able to identify jumbled and crumpled thinking? Are you able to bring about a degree of order to such thinking? Test your thinking by using the critical process.

Are you able to make a diagnosis of an issue or problem?

Are you able to recognize or identify possible risks? How do you rate yourself in the ability to take risks? I am referring to risks related to your assignment, project or task, rather than risky behavior such as running with the bulls at Pamplona, Spain.

How do you calculate the purpose and results of risks to be taken? Specifically, how can you manage risks? What about unknown risk factors or unexpected results? The critical process may be of assistance in understanding risks and risk-taking.

Are you able to recognize a struggle for power? A power play? A power grab? Are you able to recognize the abuse of authority or power? The abuse of power is the abuse of a person or persons. Using the critical process may be helpful in understanding an abuse and in understanding the issues surrounding it.

Does your thinking permit you to own your own mistakes? How do you deal with mistakes, errors in judgment or in making a decision based on a wrong conclusion?

Are you able to use your mistakes as stepping stones to find an answer, to come upon a beneficial discovery, or to uncover a new opportunity?

Keep in mind that you are judged by what and how you judge; you are evaluated by what and how you evaluate.

Reader-Thinker: What ideas do you need to add to help you to critique your own thinking process? To be helpful to yourself, be specific.

An Evaluation of the Critical Process for an Assignment, Project or Task

Reader-Thinker: Verbal accuracy and honesty are hallmarks of being a critical thinker: How do you rate yourself?

How transparent has your work been for your assignment or task? Be specific.

In using this critical process, have you fulfilled your expectations? If yes, list accomplishments. If not, why not?

If you were to begin your assignment again, using this critical process, what would you do differently? Be specific.

How can you improve this critical process in both theory and practice? Be specific.

Reflections and Suggestions for Applying Critical Thinking and a Critical Process

The following pages are added to jolt your thinking processes. They are designed to stretch your thinking and to broaden your understanding. You will find ideas, issues, reminders, insights, observations, suggestions, recommendations, examples, illustrations, commentary and bits of wisdom (I hope.) This miscellany or hodgepodge, in one way or another, relates to critical thinking and a critical process.

Etcetera: it is important to remember that the critical process is not a closed system or process, but an open one. I have used "etc." throughout this book to remind you – the Reader-Thinker – there may be something else to be considered, there may be more possibilities to be investigated, and there may be a different approach, method or system to be examined. "Etc." has been used to spike your inquisitiveness and imagination.

Be reminded...

to use the critical process, remembering that it can be adapted, and can be used along with another critical process.

to give yourself the freedom to have an open mind and to accept the challenge of dealing with new, different and diverse ideas and issues.

to ask questions, and to question your own questions.

Critical thinking is disciplined thinking.

Pursue excellence	**Aim for accuracy**
Be honest	**Be truthful**

and become worthy of trust—trustworthy.

Define: excellence, accuracy, honest/honesty, truth/truthfulness, trust/trustworthy

****

Recognize and understand the power and influence of the true, the good and the beautiful, realizing that individuals and cultures have different ways of expressing and experiencing them. How the true, the good, and the beautiful are expressed can be submitted to critical analysis.

****

Recognize and understand the complexity and the complicity of evil: question harmful, hurtful, distorted and destructive beliefs, ideas, attitudes, plans and actions. All of the aspects of hurt and harm can be expressed in a variety of ways and take different forms. These may be submitted to a critical analysis in order to understand the extent of real and possible damage and danger. It is very important to realize and to understand that the influence of evil may be at a distance – over there and out there but also nearby and here. The power and influence of negative and destructive forces and energies – over there and here – can be submitted to critical analysis for understanding.

****

Respect your conscience and the conscience of others. You may submit a declaration of conscience to a critical process as well as the issue causing a declaration of conscience to be invoked. Both positions related to conscience may be submitted to a critical process for understanding and clarification.

****

Respect differing belief systems. For example: your belief that the moon is made of green cheese does not convince me, since I believe it is made of cream cheese with diced green olives in it. The two types of cheese are open to a respectful critical analysis for understanding and clarification.

****

Raise issues of belief, morality, ethics and values, realizing that individuals have different understandings, interpretations and priorities about them. These can all be submitted to a critical process.

****

Logic is a powerful tool that can be used for understanding and clarifying issues. Keep in mind, however, that logic has also been defined as a way to go wrong with confidence, and it can be used to lead to absurdity and irrationality. History contains many ugly scenes based on the pernicious use of logic. Submit the use of this type of logic to a critical process for understanding and clarification. Give examples. Be certain to understand the logic lying beneath an ugly scene.

****

The seeming absence of an absence does not necessarily mean the absence is, in fact, absent.

To be an astute critical thinker, realize that the seeming absence of ...

philosophy or theology

political, economic and social theories

moral and ethical beliefs

law, policy, precedent or tradition

does not necessarily mean that they are absent.

Ask these questions to explore the seeming absences more deeply:

What is the philosophy or theology?

What are the political, economic and social theories?

What are the moral and ethical beliefs?

What is the law, policy, precedent or tradition?

Once a so-called absence has been identified, it can be submitted to a critical process for understanding and clarification. Give special attention to the assumptions, implications, ramifications and consequences of the noted absences.

Political, economic and social theories, moral and ethical belief systems, law, policy, precedent and tradition are not isolated one from the other. In order to understand the relationship and interaction between them, examine the relationship and interaction by using a critical process.

****

To become a proficient critical thinker, it is essential to become aware of subtle distinctions and fine points. The fine distinctions need to be brought to the light of day for examination. Be alert to, look for or point out the following, which may then be submitted to critical analysis.

Look for something causing astonishment, serendipity, wonder or mystery.

Look for a discovery that is waiting to greet you.

Look for ...

> an intention
>
> a motive
>
> mixed motives
>
> a double meaning
>
> a double standard.

Be alert to ...

> different emphases
>
> degrees of differences
>
> degrees making a difference of kind
>
> levels of intensity
>
> levels of energy
>
> levels of importance or significance.

Look for a difference that is actually a difference without merit or distinction.

Look for something that ...

is more of an opinion than a fact or truth

is plausible but might fall short in demonstration or practice

might be ineffective or weak in a practical application.

Look for ...

varying degrees of certainly and uncertainty

rhetoric that does not correspond or match the situation

moral clarity when the opposite is apparent.

Look for ...

unity

diversity

plurality.

Look for ...

cooperation

competition

harmony

disharmony

agreement

disagreement

reconciliation.

Look for what is being included or excluded.

Look for ...

opposites (apples and oranges)

the relationship of opposites

common qualities or characteristics of opposites

the attraction, interaction, tension and challenge of opposites.

Look for benchmarks, watermarks, or trademarks.

Look for an implied methodology, process or system.

Look for the implied logic of a proposition, problem or solution.

Look for a logical extension or conclusion.

Look for an exception to a rule, regulation, tradition or law, as well as an exception to an absolute. It may be helpful in understanding an exception by using the critical process.

Look for an argument based on size, longevity, or age and deal with it critically.

Look for a distinction between ...

what is basic and fundamental and what is not basic and fundamental.

what is essential and important and what is not essential and important.

what is whole or total and the parts, segments or components of the whole or total.

truth or fact and the interpretation of truth or fact.

law, policy or regulations and the interpretation of law, policy or regulation.

the individual or the group (organization, corporation, community).

Look for what is quantitative and qualitative.

Look for a tendency to ...

idealize a person, place or situation

expect perfection

create utopia – the perfect place, situation or circumstance.

Look for an argument in a circle that goes around and around. Submit such an argument to a critical process.

Look for attempts to ...

divide and conquer

bait and switch

produce a smoke screen.

Be alert to a proposition being questioned, criticized or denied that may be inherent in your own proposition, position or stance.

Be alert to greet the unexpected that may be ...

positive, beneficial, productive

negative, harmful, destructive.

Be alert to unusual expectations.

Be alert to persons who ...

are dogmatic about being undogmatic

are intolerant about being tolerant

accuse another person of being biased or prejudiced, but is unaware of his or her own biases and prejudices

accuse another person of being a hypocrite without acknowledging his or her own hypocrisy

condemn a person or group for being biased, prejudiced or hypocritical but condone or justify his or her own bias, prejudice or hypocrisy

condemn a person for being vindictive but does not face up to his or her own vindictiveness

accuse another person of something and then does the same thing

lie about or defame another person

project an idealism or perfectionism on someone so he or she can be knocked off a pedestal

build a straw man or woman so he or she can be torched

appeal to people's baser nature and interests rather than their higher and more noble attitudes and behavior

replace a doctrinaire or dogmatic statement with

another doctrinaire or dogmatic statement while claiming his or her position is neither doctrinaire nor dogmatic

retort to a rant or diatribe while believing his or her own rant or diatribe is rational

introduce an abstraction to a complex issue, assuming the abstraction is above being disputed or refuted

value things more than people

make people into things

display self-righteous certitude

take pride in their own ignorance.

Be aware of people whose arrogance overrides their logic or reason and sometimes even their common sense.

Exercise:

Look up the following words in a dictionary so you are clear about their meaning:

- bias
- prejudice
- hypocrite
- self-righteous
- ignorance
- arrogance

Be alert and point out a response or reaction that is inappropriate or disproportionate to the stimulus causing the response or reaction.

Look for, point out and deal critically with ...

predeterminism, determinism and predestinationism types of thinking

catastrophic, cataclysmic and apocalyptic types of thinking

dictatorial, authoritarian, despotic, inquisitional and brainwashing types of thinking

forced compliance or coercion.

****

Reader-Thinker: Tie a string around your finger to remember.

Remember to make the ...

profound understandable

"impossible" possible

complicated simple

difficult easy.

Remember the perfect may be the enemy of the good.

Remember to shine a searchlight into the dark and sometimes dank corners of assumptions, implications, ramifications and consequences.

Remember if something is deduced from a truth, fact or interpretation, do not assume that it necessarily applies to another truth, fact or interpretation.

Remember that people respond differently to the same people, places, things or experiences, as well as differently to different people, places, things or experiences.

Remember if something applies to one person, group or situation, do not assume that it necessarily applies to another person, group or situation.

Remember if something applies to one point in history, it does not necessarily apply to another time in history.

Remember that questions arising about identity (any type) and loyalty (any kind) need to be based on objective criteria and not on subjectivity or feelings. A critical analysis may be helpful in understanding issues surrounding identity or loyalty.

Remember to ...

locate the burden of proof for an argument or debate

ask about something lost, forgotten or omitted,

such as a footnote, reference, etc.

Remember when you make a reality check it is important to understand the reality being used for the check.

Remember to recognize and identify multiple influences and interactions. For example:

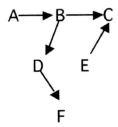

Remember to recognize and identify precedents, realizing that some precedents may take priority over other precedents.

For example:

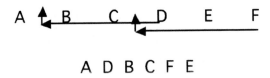

A D B C F E

Remember not to ...

offer a choice when there is no choice

let someone label or define you or your group.

****

Reader-Thinker: A *this* and *that* type of thinking does not lend itself to serious or open discussion. Many times, this kind of discourse is an over-simplification that causes a stalemate. It can be dealt with by submitting each side of a *this* or *that* argument to a critical process. In other words, deal with one side and then the other. This approach will open and clarify opposing issues that can be discussed to deepen an understanding of opposite points of view.

Examples:

Either/or

True or false

Right or wrong

Good or bad

Pro or con

Moral or immoral

Yes or no

Black or white

All or nothing

100% or 0%

One or another

Etc.

****

One person's medicine may be another person's poison.

One person's trash may be another person's treasure.

The above two popular sayings have provided the author with a model to compose the following exercise dealing with opposites and comparisons. There is no place in this task for facile distinctions and easy answers. The task is to probe and probe some more until a full understanding is ascertained, and then to explain whatever it is thoroughly and succinctly.

One person's true religion may be another person's false religion (as a political reality.)

One person's objectivity may be another person's subjectivity.

One person's light may be another person's darkness.

One person's fact may be another person's fiction.

One person's truth may be another person's falsehood.

One person's heresy may be another person's truth.

One person's belief may be another person's disbelief.

One person's opinion may be another person's belief.

One person's ideology may be another person's non-belief.

One person's rationality may be another person's irrationality.

One person's wisdom may be another person's foolishness.

One person's myth may be another person's reality.

One person's vision may be another person's illusion or delusion.

One person's good fortune may be another person's bad fortune.

One person's delight may be another person's mischief.

One person's natural experience may be another person's unnatural experience.

One person's attraction may be another person's repulsion.

One person's love may be another person's dislike or hatred.

One person's common sense may be another person's nonsense.

One person's doing the right thing may be another person's doing the wrong thing.

One person's morality may be another person's immorality.

One person's ought may be another person's ought not.

One person's harmony may be another person's disharmony.

One person's life-enhancing experience may be another person's life-diminishing experience.

One person's relevancy may be another person's irrelevancy.

One person's liberalism may be another person's conservatism.

One person's conservatism may be another person's liberalism.

One person's moderate position may be another person's extreme position.

One person's progress may be another person's regression.

One person's reform may be another person's

needless change.

One person's freedom may be another person's slavery.

One person's liberty may be another person's restraint and deterrence.

One person's justice may be another person's injustice.

One person's friend may be another person's enemy.

One person's hero may be another person's villain.

One person's patriotic deed or idea may be another person's unpatriotic act or idea.

One person's patriot may be another person's traitor.

One person's terrorist may be another person's freedom fighter.

One person's dead terrorist may be another person's martyr.

One person's evil society may be another person's good society.

Just War Theory: One person's just (or justified) war may be another person's unjust war.

****

One person's power or authority may need protection from another person's power or authority.

One person's truth may need protection from another person's truth.

One person's conscience may need protection from another person's conscience.

One person's values and principles may need protection from another person's values and principles.

One person's freedom may need protection from another person's freedom.

One person's freedom of religion may need protection from another person's freedom of religion.

One person's freedom of speech may need protection from another person's freedom of speech.

One group's freedom of assembly may need protection from another group's freedom of assembly.

One group's freedom of the press may need protection from another group's freedom of the press.

Reader-Thinker: you may use your own critical and analytical skills to give examples. Then an example may be submitted to the critical process for understanding and clarification.

****

To be a fair interpreter of a person's life, it is important not to categorize a person (or group) by a single statement, activity or event. For example, interpret a person's life or contribution to history in a comprehensive and inclusive way, neither ignoring nor denying some negative statement, activity or event. The issue is to balance and to weigh all aspects of a person's life when interpreting it.

****

A belief in freedom grants a person the privilege for changing his or her mind, changing his or her thinking about ideas, issues, purposes, policies, plans, etc.

(1) John Doe has changed his thinking about A and now endorses B. By using the critical process A can be analyzed, clarified and understood.

(2) John Doe has the obligation to explain the reasons for the change from A to B. His explanations or reasons for the change need to be thorough and complete. His intelligence, integrity,

honesty and truthfulness can be critically analyzed and evaluated.

(3) Then B (whatever it is) can be submitted to
the critical process to be analyzed, clarified and
understood.

(4) By using this outline, John Doe's change of
mind from A to B can be fully evaluated and a
judgment can be made about his change of
thinking.

****

If you hear someone announce that he or she believes
in certain principles and values, make sure you examine
his or her profession of belief. Do not settle for abstractions.

Be certain to enquire about the principles and
values; they must be specified and be specific.

The principles and values then may be examined
by submitting them to the critical process.

Once the principles and values are understood
and clarified, they may be used to match the
person's attitudes, behavior and actions with the
principles and values he or she has professed to
believe in and live by.

****

If you encounter a seemingly airtight argument, category or classification, perhaps it can be pried open by asking a probing question. For example, a conservative (of any discipline or persuasion) may be asked what he or she might like to liberalize or liberate. In turn, a liberal (of any discipline or persuasion) may be asked what he or she might like to conserve. The responses may then be submitted to a critical process for understanding and clarification.

****

The Rule of Law is a noble tradition undergirding both civility and stability in society. However, the Rule of Law should never be used as a cover or as an excuse for unjust, unfair and mean-spirited purposes. Laws in general and, especially, unjust and unfair laws should be submitted to a critical analysis and process for understanding and clarification.

****

When you hear someone expressing his or her feelings that the nation, corporation, business, family or individual is going in the wrong direction, first of all respect the statement of his or her feelings of worry, fear or depression. It is important, however, to go beyond the feelings and test the reasons accompanying the feelings.

What are the concerns, issues, policies, plans, programs,

etc. causing the feelings? By using the critical process, the feelings may be interpreted and clarified

****

Political and social labels are frequently used to identify individuals and groups as

liberal

progressive

conservative

right

left

center or moderate.

The issue is not so much that a person is liberal, progressive, conservative, etc. as it is what he or she is...

liberal about

progressive about

conservative about.

Then the problem, idea, issue, plan, project or policy may be examined by using the critical process to understand and clarify whatever is being considered or debated.

Also, it is important to use specific and verifiable

criteria when you label a person or group as being liberal, conservative, right, left, etc. Accuracy of terminology is necessary when applying labels to a person or group. Critical thinking requires this.

****

Economic and political incantations: Sometimes the following words are used as if they were incantations. That is, if you repeat them one hundred times, they will define themselves; and then, if you say them another hundred times, they will automatically solve issues and problems.

Democracy

Capitalism

Free market, free enterprise

Socialism

Communism

Marxism

Fascism

National self-interest

American way or dream

Patriotism

Freedom

Liberty

And similar words.

These words defy simplified explanations, oblique generalizations, or glib pronouncements. There is no substitute for a complete understanding and accurate knowledge. These and similar political and economic terms need to be fully understood and clarified by using the critical process. Again, verbal accuracy is important.

****

If there is reason to believe that a witch hunt or contemporary inquisition is being planned or is actually underway, it is of paramount importance to respond by submitting it to the critical process.

It is essential to identify and examine whatever is being used to define, fuel and feed the witch hunt or inquisition and deal with it critically.

In understanding this type of activity, there needs to be an analysis of the sources, assumptions, implications, ramifications and consequences of a witch hunt or contemporary inquisition.

****

It is important to be vigilant in watching for assumed or implied punitive measures (punishments) that may be or are already being applied to individuals and groups for some reason or in some circumstance. Be especially astute in bringing punitive measures – existing, assumed or implied – into daylight. All need to be examined by using the critical process.

****

Change is constant. Change is defined as altering, modifying or making something different.

Some people like change and accept the challenge of it. Others may be neutral about it. Still others may not like and even hate it. Some individuals may be traumatized by it. There are some people who may like some parts of a change but not other parts of it.

How well you understand, explain, interpret and manage a change may determine the success of an assignment, project or task.

The following is a basic outline of some of the issues revolving around change.

Understand ...

the nature and purpose of a change or changes.

the change itself.

the issues surrounding the change.

the intellectual (objective) responses to it.

the emotional (subjective) responses to it.

the value systems, value judgments and other considerations associated with a change.

Pay particular attention to a conflict of values relating to a change.

And pay particular attention to a conflict over expectations related to a change.

Is there a possibility of a backlash related to a change? If so, how can you prepare yourself for a possible backlash?

Each of the above listed points may be submitted to a critical process in attempting to understand and clarify a change or changes.

Thoughts and a Challenge

Miles and miles of library shelves are lined with biographies telling the stories of men and women, young and old, whose lives are testimonies of

Thinking

Doing.

History is illumined by individuals known for their profound and innovative thinking in the universe of ideas and by their deeds, works and service. To be a creative and critical thinker may bring recognition, accolades, promotion and rewards.

Remember also that from the first pages of history to the present, fellow human beings have been killed, crucified, assassinated, burned at the stake, hanged from trees, stoned, shot, tortured, mutilated, beaten, poisoned, ostracized, shunned, denigrated, marginalized, imprisoned, fined, banished and expelled because of their

Thinking
Doing.

Be aware of consequences – both positive and negative – for being a creative and critical thinker.

The challenge is to apply the power of critical thinking to all ideas, situations and circumstances.

Therefore...

Critical Thinker:

Take courage

to dare to think and

to dare to do and to act.

About the Author

Donald L. Karshner grew up in Columbus, Ohio and was educated in the Columbus public schools. He earned a Bachelor of Arts degree and a Master of Education degree from the Ohio State University in Columbus, and taught school for three years in Columbus.

Karshner went on to earn a Master of Divinity degree from Union Theological Seminary in New York City. He is a priest of the Episcopal church. For thirty years, he served parishes in Massachusetts, Ohio and Delaware. At age 87, he is retired and makes his home in Philadelphia, PA.

CPSIA information can be obtained at www.ICGtesting.com
Printed in the USA
LVOW06s1644300715

448251LV00002BA/345/P